KICK THE LATCH

Kathryn Scanlan

This edition first published in the
United Kingdom in 2023 by
Daunt Books Originals
83 Marylebone High Street
London W1U 4QW

2

First published in 2022 by New Direction Books, New York

AUTHOR'S NOTE
Thank you to Teresa Scanlan, George Scanlan, Caleb Lyons,
Harriet Moore, Marigold Atkey, Jimena Gorráez and Daunt Books
for their support in the creation and publication of this book.
Thank you to Barbara Epler and New Directions for publishing it
in the US in 2022. Thank you to Emily Stokes and the *Paris Review*
for printing an excerpt in the Spring 2022 issue, to *Harper's* for
excerpting it in their August 2022 issue, and to Rachael Allen and
Granta for publishing an excerpt on the magazine's website.
And to Sonia—thank you for the conversations.

A CIP catalogue record for this title is available from the British Library.

ISBN 978-1-914198-25-0

Typeset by Marsha Swan
Printed and bound by TJ Books Ltd, Padstow, Cornwall

www.dauntbookspublishing.co.uk

To Sonia

1

SOLID PLASTER

I was born October 1st, 1962. I was born in Dixon City, Iowa. I was born with a dislocated hip. The doctor said I'd never walk. My mom said, Oh no, there's got to be something. So they put me in solid plaster from my chest down, with just a little spot for my mom to put a diaper. I was in there five months. Then I went to two casts on my legs with a bar in between with these special shoes. Ended up I could walk. I attribute that to Dr. Johnson. My mom always said, Well, if it wasn't for Dr. Johnson.

THE OLD MAN

We lived in a poor part of town but we had the greatest entertainment. We had the goldfish ponds, we had Motorcycle Hill, we had the dump and Bicycle Jenny. We made rafts for the creek. We lived off the land.

Down the street was a family who'd moved off the reservation —grandfather and kids and grandkids. The grandkids were our age and we spent a lot of time with them. The grandfather liked to tell me about his religion, his beliefs. I loved his stories and his tales. I called him Grandpa.

The old man—he was very well loved but he liked to drink. His daughter and her husband locked him out of the house when he got drunk. I'd say, Grandpa can stay with us—I'll sleep in my sister's room so Grandpa can have mine. So the old man would stay in my room and he'd go home when he sobered up.

His daughter and her husband didn't like Grandpa to drink but they drank, too. They'd drink and get into fights and their kids would come over and we'd call the police. We'd watch out the bedroom window when the police came and hauled them off in handcuffs. The husband was carted away on a stretcher once for stab wounds.

IT WASN'T HIS FAULT

When I was six we got a big dog, but the dog kept wrapping his legs around me and taking my pants off in the front yard. It wasn't his fault—he wasn't fixed and I was the right height.

A week later my mom sent the dog back to the man who gave it to us. I cried like crazy when I came home and the dog was gone.

Then my uncle knew a man getting rid of a Shetland pony, but it was a stallion. Uncle borrowed a trailer anyway and brought the stallion pony to our house. We lived in a cheap rental with a rickety little white picket fence. We tied the pony to a concrete block in the front yard where there was plenty of grass to eat.

One day some girls rode by on their mares and the stallion pony started hollering his mating demand. I grabbed his halter but he kicked me against the side of the house. My mom picked up the concrete block to stop him but instead she went skidding down the road behind him—asphalt skiing. Finally a driver pulled over to help and they dragged the pony home together. My mom was scraped and bumped and black and blue all over.

The pony went away right after that.

MILK BONES

The neighbor girl who was my age, Regina—we lived on dog biscuits, Milk Bones. We ate slices of bread from the bag.

No one was there in the morning when I got ready for school. I'd put on my mom's red lipstick and her dresses and her high-heeled shoes.

In first grade, eight girls had me up against the lockers, saying, Punch her, punch her! I didn't want to fight, but when one of them came at me I kicked off my heels and let her have it.

They took us to the principal's office and later my mom showed up. There were scratches on the girl's face and she had a black eye. I thought they would put me in prison. My mom said, Are those my shoes?

BICYCLE JENNY

Before her husband died and her house burned down, Bicycle Jenny worked at Crocker's, the slaughtering plant. What was left of her house was a scorched concrete hole in the ground. That's where she lived.

She rode a bicycle with a little cart on the back for carrying sacks of oatmeal from town. She'd stop by our house on the way because we had a lot of dandelion greens in our yard. She'd pick them and cook them up.

She wore men's shirts, bright red lipstick, bright red rouge. Her face was real weathered, wind-burnt. She wasn't very big but she was kind of stocky. In summer she wore a kerchief on her head and in winter she wore wool hats, a hood, layers on layers, big men's coats, men's warm boots.

She was the best gardener. Dr. Cheltington and some others in the rich neighborhood hired her to do their grounds work. She could make anything grow and those yards were gorgeous because of her.

If she came into your house, you'd still smell her a day later. When the weather was warm she bathed in the creek or ponds, but in winter she reeked. Most of the boys in the neighborhood, the first naked woman they seen was Bicycle Jenny taking a bath in the goldfish ponds.

She had a lot of dogs—little yipping chihuahuas—and a chicken wire fence to keep them in. I'm talking sixty, seventy chihuahuas without stretching it a bit. She always said she had a hundred.

When we saw her head off to town, we'd go over there. We'd get through the fence and past the dogs and walk around looking at things. She had clothes-pins and wire hanging from trees. Down in her hole in the ground was an old-fashioned bathtub and a little cast-iron camp stove. She had test tubes with rubber stoppers, little blue bottles, jars of jellies she made from her raspberry bushes. She had some bright red berries, too. Someone said they were probably poison.

Bicycle Jenny had the go-ahead, anytime she needed water, to come into our house and get it. She'd fill her cream cans in our sink and carry them back on her wagon. When it was snowy she used a sled.

If our parents were home we weren't afraid of her, but if she showed up when they were gone, we were. My sister and I would see her coming and hide under the bed. We'd wait and listen for the front door to open.

She talked to herself while she filled up at the sink. Her voice was high, cracked, eerie like a witch's. She had her big men's work gloves, her hat and her other hat, and she'd usually have some chihuahuas stuffed in her coat.

Bicycle Jenny would say, Look what I've got, and she'd pull them out of her shirt pocket. She kept the puppies in little strawberry baskets.

One summer a stray cat turned up at our house and had babies. There was a sickly little orange one with a head that wobbled back and forth. When it was just off the titty I showed it to Bicycle Jenny and said, Look at my little kitten, there's something wrong with its head. She said, Let me take her, see what I can do.

I thought, We'll never see that kitten again. I kind of forgot about it. I guess I had other cats. I don't remember worrying about it or wondering. I don't know how much time went by—maybe a few weeks. But then Bicycle Jenny showed up when I was lying out in the hammock and said, Somebody wants to see you.

I don't know what she did, I don't know how she kept her little dogs from killing it, but the cat was fine and its head no longer shook. She didn't swap kittens—this cat was orange with three distinct white marks. No two cats have the same markings.

A few months later, my sister and I were raking leaves with our mom when an ambulance went by, then cop cars. There wasn't much traffic on our street and we were nosy—we ran over there. We heard screaming and crying and dogs barking. There was a whole string of emergency personnel. They said she wasn't taking care of herself. People can't live like that, they said. It took several large men to get her into the ambulance. The dogs were running everywhere, getting chased with long-handled nets. We were screaming and crying, too.

They hauled her off to a home at Comstock, Iowa. I always wanted to go up to Comstock to see her. She lived at the home a long time. She was close to a hundred years old when she died.

I still have the newspaper clipping with her obituary. My mom kept it in a scrapbook. Her name was Marla Weaver. She was originally from Chesterfield, I believe.

Down in her hole in the ground were piles and piles of blankets and sleeping bags for Bicycle Jenny. But those dogs—chihuahuas are little thin-haired things—how'd they not freeze in the winter? I didn't think nothing of it when I was a kid but I'm thinking of it now—how'd the dogs survive?

If somebody told me this story, I'd definitely say, You're fucking nuts. Chihuahuas? In a hole? In the wintertime, in a bathtub? In Iowa?

2

THE JOCKEY

At school, everyone wondered what you wanted to do when you grew up. I said I wanted to be a jockey, riding racehorses. The teachers were concerned. But jockeys are small, and I was getting tall. People told me, Put books on your head, you won't grow. So I'd be walking around with books. I stacked the heaviest ones I could find.

My parents took us to the racetrack in Jackson on weekends. My dad would go inside to gamble and my mom'd wait outside with my sister and me. We'd lean on the rail and watch them run.

THERE WAS NOTHING ELSE

Well what do you want for Christmas and what do you want for your birthday and what is it you would like, as a treat?

A horse!

We had no permission, no money, but my sister and I rode our bicycles to all the neighbors' houses to ask: Do you have any horses for sale or do you know of any place we could keep a horse or do you know anyone who does have a horse for sale and if so how much?

Keith Baxter owned a stable in Dixon City where you could rent a horse by the hour. The first time my mom took me there, Baxter put me on a giant horse named Joe. I said, I want to ride that one instead—and I pointed at a little horse off by himself in the corral. Baxter said, If you can't ride Joe you sure as heck ain't gonna ride Rowdy.

BANG!

Rowdy was a little mustang out of Black River, North Dakota — a paint, brown and white, just beautiful. We had a connection. He was always my pick to ride.

Melvyn Abernathy was a well-known trick rider in Dixon City with a team of palominos. What Melvyn did was drive out to Black River and round up a bunch of wild horses from the range and load them into his trailer. Melvyn brought Rowdy home.

When Melvyn tried to work with the horse, Rowdy kept getting loose — Melvyn's fences were too short — so he sold him to Keith Baxter. But Rowdy wasn't popular at Baxter's either — he unseated everyone who tried to ride him. I fell off plenty of times but I got right back on.

You see the old pictures of the cowboy and the dog — they look like they're asleep — and the horse is plodding along. Rowdy wasn't like that. As soon as he thought you weren't paying attention — bang! you'd be on the ground. He was nervous and quick. He'd spook. He was sensitive. It was his heritage.

I HAD MY SPILLS

He was a small horse, so I didn't have far to fall. First I rode him in Baxter's big arena. I'd fall off and get back on and Baxter would be shaking his head. Then one day Baxter said, Okay, you can go down the road now. I'd ride with a group of people from the stable in ditches along the highway. Cars with loud mufflers went by and Rowdy unseated me. Pheasants popped up from the brush and I got unseated.

Rowdy'd unseat me and run back to Baxter's, but when I got tired of walking three miles to the stable or riding double on another gal's horse, I learned how to stay on. I paid attention to his twitching ears and the feel of his body. When he tensed up, I talked to him. I couldn't afford a saddle so I rode bareback, which strengthens your legs and gives you balance.

Anytime I mowed grass or did jobs around the house, my folks forked over the dollar so I could ride Rowdy. If I had no money I'd go just to brush him and talk to him.

Once, on my birthday, I got to rent him for five hours straight. We packed a little lunch, the horse and I did, and went out to the pasture to run around. Rowdy kneeled in the grass and I jumped off. He pawed in the crick and rolled in the water. We ate our treats and napped in the shade of a big tree.

MY PAINT HORSE

One day Keith Baxter said, You know, I'm going to sell that horse. He said he'd sell him for a hundred dollars.

I ran home and cleaned the house, trying to suck up big-time before my mom got off work. She worked really hard and my dad worked really hard—he was a Korea War vet. They paid seventy-five dollars a month to rent the house we lived in.

My mom said, Ask your father. My dad said, In a week you'll be sick of him—you'll be chasing boys instead.

Then my mom asked Gary Goldberg what he thought. Gary was a great horseman with a stable in Storyville, a few miles away. If it was too hot or the flies were bad, Gary'd refuse to rent you a horse, whereas Keith Baxter was happy to take your money. To my mom, Gary Goldberg said, I don't think it's a good idea.

A week later I was riding Rowdy, crying—I thought it was the last time I'd see him. Baxter and my mom were watching me from the side of the corral. Then Baxter cupped his hand around his mouth and yelled, Well, what do you think of your new horse?

After that there were boarding bills to pay—we kept him at Keith's—and feed and tack and vet bills, too. My mom, she sacrificed a lot of her own little life so that I—I had to get the horse.

KIND OF FUNNY, A REAL CLOWN, AN ORNERY SON OF A BUCK

Any chance I had I was headed to Baxter's. We'd get out of class early in a blizzard and I was on my way in the snow. Five miles out—I rode my bike until somebody stole it. Then I walked or hitched a ride with other people from the stable.

The school would call my mom and tell her I was missing. She knew to check Baxter's first. There I'd be on my paint horse, riding down the road with a big smile on my face.

If I was in a good mood, Rowdy might test me. If I was in a hurry, he wouldn't let me catch him. He taught me trust. He taught me not to trust too much. I learned to be a little leery.

The other girls at the stable could use the hose on their horses but I had to give Rowdy a sponge bath with a five-gallon bucket of water. He never got used to the hose—it sounded like a snake.

My horse could tell if I was having a bad day. If I was sitting in the stall or out in the pasture crying, he'd nudge me with his head until I started laughing. If I was riding him and thought, I want to go a little faster, he'd go a little faster. He was always looking at me—and I'd be looking back at him.

If your parents don't get along, if they argue, if there's an abuse situation, you've got your horse. When things were bad I'd go to the horse and the horse would always make it better. That's why I always say my horse raised me.

3

A LITTLE WIND-UP CLOCK

When I was sixteen I wrote letters to horse trainers and racetracks. I got their names and addresses from the racing programs I'd collected. I told them I would work for room and board to learn the ropes.

I got a call from an outfit in Denton, Iowa—BT Beauregard, Buford Beauregard and his brother Lester. They had three thoroughbreds and a quarter horse. I lived with them on their farm all summer while school was out—Bud and Lester and their friend Riley Walker from Tindall.

I learned how to run bandages and how to put a mud knot in a horse's tail. I learned to massage their legs to get the blood going.

I had a little wind-up clock. When they said to rub each leg for five minutes, I had my clock to make sure I did.

I had a favorite horse—Buckin' Bones was his name. Oh, I loved that horse. I loved all my horses. I spent the day always with the horses. Everybody called me Bones.

SHORT-IRON

I learned to gallop around the cornfields. There was always pheasants or deer jumping up to spook the thoroughbreds. I was riding short-iron, jockey-style. You use a light little saddle with a flat cantle and you stand in your irons—it takes the weight off the horse's back and puts it over his loin and shoulders. You use long reins and tie them—you make a special cross. Lester's daughter taught me how to make my cross and to keep my shoulders right, my back straight. You think about balance and control and you go easy on their mouths—you use a ring bit or snaffle bit, kind bits, not severe.

There's an art to knowing how much horse you have left under you. You might get out in front in a route race, but you'll run out of gas. No horse can run full bore the whole time. When you train a route horse, you do long, slow gallops to instill air in him. You make sure he has enough to carry him through to the end.

DIRT TRACK, FLAT LAND, RAMSHACKLE BACKSTRETCH

When we put a horse in to race at Jackson, South Dakota, I got to go along. We'd haul in the night before, sleep in a stall at the racetrack, and run our horse the next day. I rode in Old Bud's pickup, in the middle, with Bud on one side and Riley Walker on the other. Old Bud would be puffing away on his nasty cigars and I'd be gagging. We pulled the trailer behind us and when we arrived, our stalls were ready—one for the horse, one for Bud, one for Riley, and one for me.

I'd been to Park Jackson plenty with my parents, but now I was on the backside. I got to meet other racetrack people besides those Denton people. I stood in the winner's circle with Buckin' Bones and got my picture taken.

Park Jackson was a recognized track, the only parimutuel betting in the state, but it was bottom of the barrel—one step above the bushes. It was backwoodsy. All kinds of crap went on.

Still, it was where some good horses, some good trainers got their start.

Of course it's gone now. They race motorcycles there instead.

I WOULDN'T BARELY BREAK

I went home at the end of the season. School started, but in my free time I read every book I could find about racehorses— feeding and conditioning and interval training and selective breeding and line breeding and hoof care, anatomy. I wanted to be better prepared when I went back.

The next summer Bud and Lester put me in charge at Park Jackson—I kept their horses for them on the racetrack grounds. Sometimes I had four horses, sometimes three. I was there all week, alone. I did everything. They gave me a workout schedule and I carried out the orders. On weekends they'd drive up from Denton for the races.

Did quite well. Very successful. We were in the money— meaning first, second, third, or fourth place—at least sixty-five, seventy percent of the time, which is phenomenal.

I lived in a trailer park with other racetrackers. My trailer was a mile, mile and a quarter out. Four o'clock feed—I didn't have a car. I'd start walking across a field in the dark at three fifteen in the morning.

I worked all day at the track. Never left. Most people did. I wouldn't barely break to go to the track kitchen to get a bite to eat and I was right back with the horses. People, they knew I was dedicated.

I was known as the Coca-Cola kid because everyone wanted to buy me a drink, get me drunk, but I'd ask for soda instead. Not to say I never overdid it—but it was rare. You say okay to one drink, then suddenly you've got twenty more in front of you, and twenty people telling you to swallow it.

NOTHING NICE

Those racetrack trailers were run-down, really dilapidated—
nothing nice.

A goose lived there. As soon as you stepped out your door
the goose would come and—bam!—she'd nail you in the back
of the leg.

There were goats. One day I was sick, lying down with the door
open because it was so hot—no air-conditioning, just a fan—and
when I woke up, a goat was next to me, chewing on my sleeve.

My bedroom looked out on a cow pen and at night I'd listen
to them moo.

Whenever it rained, there'd be water everywhere pouring
down—fucking bucket bucket bucket, pails pails pails.

My mom and dad came to visit after I got my finger half
bitten off by a horse. When they first got there, my dad was busy
poking around. He said, What the hell is a butcher knife doing
sitting in the window?

Well, I had these knives. I had this butcher knife. I kept it handy. You never know.

KEY TO THE QUARTER POLE

When you're a greenhorn and eager to learn, someone might say, Why don't you go over to Barn Six and ask if you can borrow their saddle stretcher? So you go to Barn Six and say, Biff Gifford wants to know if he can borrow your saddle stretcher, and the person at Barn Six says, I gave it to Barn Nine, you can get it from them. You go to Barn Nine, but the person there sends you to Barn Twelve and says, While you're at it, can you get me the key to the quarter pole? You're walking back and forth, barn to barn, but there's no such thing as a saddle stretcher or quarter-pole key.

One guy knew I was afraid of mice, so he'd catch them and put them in my feed sack. At four o'clock in the morning, half-awake, I'd pull up the lid and put my hand into the sack and six mice would jump onto my arm. I'd be screaming and he'd be laughing.

They stick one horse in another horse's stall to get you flustered, or they take your horse, put him on a walker, and say,

Where'd your horse go, where'd your horse go? They mess with you, especially when you're new, and then pretty soon you're doing it to people, too.

GALLON OF BLOOD

At Park Jackson it was the cheaper horses, but a lot of them were at one time big-money horses. In the past they ran for forty, fifty thousand dollars, but most were so broke down you could buy them for fifteen hundred in a claiming race.

Most racehorses bleed from the lungs when they run. They won't win because they're choking on the blood coming up. There was a drug you'd use to bring their blood pressure down, but then that drug got banned because it could mask other drugs.

Some of the old-timers at Park Jackson would tie smooth wire tight to the root of the tail to constrict blood flow. Others took blood from the neck with a big syringe and squirted it into a milk jug until the jug was full. Sometimes the jug got knocked over—there'd be blood all over the ground.

One trainer in particular liked to do it. He plunged so many syringes people would joke, Hey Joey, how come your right thumb's so much bigger than your left?

NUTS AND BOLTS

The horses got the best feed, they loved to run, but some of them were pieced together with nuts and bolts. Their legs—you call them their wheels. This horse has a bad wheel. There might be a screw holding the bones together. There might be a knee swollen the size of my head. You tell the rider, Don't look down, jock!

If a horse breaks a leg, it usually gets euthanized. Sometimes their legs detach. Not to say you can't fix a broken leg or even one that's busted off. They've done wonders with big-money horses— some have prosthetics. But it's not always humane. If it's a gelding or a horse worth only a grand, you can't go to great lengths to save them because it will cost too much.

I was seven the first time I seen a horse break down on the racetrack. I watched it get injected. Then the crew hooked the dead horse to an old tractor with a log chain and dragged it off the track in front of everybody. That was in 1969 at Park Jackson.

Now they use an ambulance. They pull a big curtain from the trailer and the horse gets loaded up—even with a broken leg it'll stumble in. They haul the horse to the backside and do what they have to do.

BIG OLD HOLE

Sometimes three or four horses would break down in one race because the track surface at Park Jackson wasn't up to par and a lot of the horses were too crippled up to be racing in the first place. There was a reservation close by and if ever a gray horse had to be put down, the Winnebagos would come and take off the tail. They'd dye the hair and make it for their costume.

The rendering truck came every other Monday. In the meantime the corpses would pile up in a drainage ditch behind the grandstand. Every day, on the way from my trailer to the barn and back again, I had to pass this big old hole. The horses' legs would be sticking straight up in the air, and the smell—

One Saturday while I was riding a Beauregard horse from the barn to the starting gate for a race, I glanced over at the drainage ditch. A horse had been euthanized earlier that day after a bad fall, but now that horse was trying to stand up. It was struggling because both of its front legs were broken. The other pony people turned to see what I was staring at. Oh my god, someone said, it's still alive. The vet didn't put it down right. We had to call him back so he could finish the job.

Priests came on race days to bless the horses' legs before they ran, but there'd be plenty of times it didn't work.

I SEEN HIM EVERY DAY

Near the end of summer, I woke up in my trailer one night with a man over me. He sneaked in while I was sleeping and put a gun to my head. I got raped.

He was taking pills. He was a jockey trying to cut weight. He told me he'd just shot a dog.

I didn't say anything because if I'd said something, I would've been off the track. My folks would've come and got me.

The guy sobered up, I knew him, I seen him every day, I knew exactly who it was—it was bad, but anyway, I survived. I cut my hair real short after that.

4

PICKLED BOILED EGGS

Turned eighteen, finished school, got my diploma. Went full-time at the racetrack. Instead of working one racetrack I traveled the circuit with my racetrack family. There was grooms, jockeys, trainers, racing secretaries, stewards, pony people, hot walkers, everybody. When one meet ended we'd all go down the road together, bumper-to-bumper. We'd go to the same grocery stores, the same laundromats.

We'd go to a bar after the races and it'd be a racetrack bar—the locals would leave. We didn't want anyone else around. Sometimes it ended in a brawl, but usually we landed on our feet. We even had our own band—the Bug Boys. The singer was a jockey, the drummer was a trainer, the bass player was a groom.

Not everybody drank—some just liked to mingle and talk. We'd gather at long tables and watch replays of the races, the whole card on loop. Oh, see—right there! What did I tell him? I told him not to go to the outside, and what'd he do? See his head bobble?

One night an exercise rider brought his bulldog to the bar. The dog jumped into our booth and people started buying it pickled boiled eggs from a big jar. The dog loved them and everyone liked this dog, so everyone bought the dog a pickled boiled egg, but there are only so many pickled boiled eggs a dog can eat before there are consequences to clean up.

THANKSGIVING

People didn't want to rent to us because we'd be in town only a few months and because racetrackers tend to be wild and destroy apartments. I'd stay in a trailer, a motel room, a stall at the track. Sometimes I lived out of my truck. I didn't have a TV for years and years. I didn't have time to watch TV, nor did I really want to. Never did cook much because I didn't have a home.

For breakfast, everyone heads to the track kitchen—you don't travel to town to eat. Each track kitchen was known for a special dish. One had homemade donuts. There'd be scrambled eggs, bacon. For dinner you might order a hamburger at the bar—whatever they have.

A track in Nebraska sold Polish dogs to spectators on race days. Weekends it was all you could smell—the strong dogs with onions and sauerkraut. The meat was kept in unlocked coolers in the grandstand, and one night a bunch of racetrackers ransacked them. When the weekend came, there was no Polish dogs to sell because the racetrackers stole every one. They'd soaked them in beer and put them on the grill and had a big party.

At Park Jackson, there were four jockeys who lived together in a trailer. They got a deer out of season once and butchered it in their bathtub. They made venison jerky and shared it.

For a few months I was renting a room at the El Rancho Motel for $211 a week, and on Thanksgiving the creep I lived with cooked a turkey in an electric roaster in the bathroom. He propped the roaster on the sink next to the high-voltage outlet. It was the moistest turkey I've ever eaten.

ENOUGH

The backside is a little city. You flash your track license at the guard shack to get in. There's an ambulance on the grounds during training hours because people are always getting hurt. Feed dealers sell sawdust, straw, oats, beet pulp, bran, good hay. Tack wagons stock bandages, saddles, medication, leg paints, sweats, freezes, Bowie Clay, sheet cotton, vet wrap. You live at the track, your life is full. You don't have time to go shopping at the mall. You lose touch with the outside. Things change. You don't hear about world news unless something major happens, because you're in your own world and you have enough news.

CALL YOUR OWNERS,
CALL HOME

No cell phones then—had to use pay phones. Had to have bags of change handy always. I'd plug it in and dial and wait. Call your owners, call home, it was hard—after your horse ran you'd call your owner if your owner hadn't shown up for the race.

Stupid pay booth, phone booth. We'd be at a restaurant and all the other trainers would be trying to call their owners, too. Finally it's your turn and it feels like you're dialing and talking forever. You want to get to bed because you've got to get up at four to feed. Here it is 8:30 and you can't get through—nobody's answering, there's a busy signal—and you still have to water off and get something to eat and do laundry.

When I went full-time at the track, I always had that on my shoulders—you're not there to help your sister, you're not there for your folks, you're not there for holidays, birthdays, weddings, doctor's appointments, funerals. I paid Keith Baxter to take care of Rowdy for me. I saw him once a year, at Christmas.

HAMBURGERS

A jockey took me out to a movie once, but I fell asleep in the first ten minutes. Jockeys get their naps in—they're galloping and working the horses at five o'clock in the morning, but after that they can leave, do what they want. The rest of us—a lot of us—were there twelve, fourteen, sixteen hours a day.

Last dash of a night race ends around 7:30, but you don't just feed the horse and throw him in a stall—you've got to cool him out, walk him, water him off, do up his legs, put him in ice or in a tub. By the time you're done, it's midnight, 12:30.

One night after last dash I went home, didn't even eat—I was exhausted and had to be up again at four. I was renting a room from an old lady who knew the people I worked for. I lay down, slept, got up, got dressed, went back to the track. No one else was there except for a guy grilling hamburgers near my barn. What time is it? I asked him. It's 2:30, he said.

Sometimes my folks would come to the races and we'd go out to eat afterwards. It'd be eight o'clock at night and I couldn't even talk. I'd be falling asleep on the table.

OUR PERSONAL ATTITUDES

You get hit. I got kicked in the head. The horse was kicking at a fly and my head got in the way. Riders would go down. They'd get steel rods put up their spine. You were on top of the world or the bottom. You'd get hurt and be laid up with no money coming in, but there'd be other weeks where you made real good.

It's a sport, you're competitive—you want to be tops, you want to win, you want your name on the program, in the standings. A trainer'll try to swipe an owner from another trainer. A jockey'll say to another jockey—What the fuck are you doing, sniffing around my stable? Bad feelings, hard feelings, friction—nobody loves everybody. But if someone gets hurt, laid up, down on their luck, loses a loved one—even if their truck breaks down on the way to the next track—we'd work together to help. We'd have a big benefit.

I'd pull manes—ten mane jobs, ten sheath cleanings—and the money that would've been my fee would go into the pot.

When I got hurt, people covered for me. They fed my horses and got them out to exercise. We stuck together.

The racetrack chaplain, he'd make rounds. Everything going okay? He was concerned about the backside, our personal attitudes, problems, hard times we were having, good times. If we wanted to talk, he was available. The chaplain'd say, We're having a service tonight, seven o'clock under the grandstands. We'd be dirty in our work clothes but he'd say, Just come as you are, we'd love to have you. And he'd make sure the service was held after our chores were done. It wouldn't be on a Sunday because there was races on Sundays. It'd be on a dark day in the middle of the week.

Before a race card started, the chaplain would hold a prayer service in the jockeys' room. A lot of the jocks joined. Most of them—I think all of them—would sit and say a prayer together. It didn't matter what they believed.

5

I OUTGREW THE POSITION

I met the jockeys and seen what they did to make weight. They slap on glycerin and cling-wrap and sit in their cars with the heater blasting when it's a hundred in the shade—they pass out. They go in the hot-box—it's like a refrigerator with a spot on top for your head to stick out. Once, a jock caught on fire when the hotbox short-circuited. He had terrible burns all over his body.

The jockeys flip their food or they don't eat at all. They get so good at puking they brag about it—*I can flip the rice but leave the beans!*

For a few weeks I stopped eating, thinking I could shrink myself. But I was tall—though we do have some tall jocks—and I was muscular doing all that work. The jocks are muscular too of course but they're smaller-statured. There was no way I could keep it up without getting sick.

Sometimes a jockey hasn't ever been on the back of the horse he's riding. They don't develop a close relationship. I loved to gallop the racehorses, and I ponied, too. I got to work them, open them up, breeze them. I took them to the starting gates. I did everything a jockey does except ride in a race.

THEY GET CHILLY

Some riders sit on a horse like you could balance an egg on their back and they wouldn't lose it, or a saucer of milk and they wouldn't spill a drop. They're subtle and gentle. A cowboy type is what you want for a horse who's really rough, kind of rank. Other jockeys are good with a stick—they can switch hands sticking while they ride. But a lot of horses quit if you hit them. There's jockeys that have a hell of a hand and they bring them horses home with welts. If a horse is running full bore why do you need to stick him?

Jocks get thrown, get hurt, sometimes bad. When that happens, they can get chilly. They're afraid to get on a horse. They have flashbacks. They have to prove themselves again and again. Everyone's watching to see what they'll do.

THIS JOCK PACKS, THAT JOCK PACKS

A little hotshot machine like a flat battery, two-pronged, pocket-size—a jockey will use it to shock his horse. He hides it down the front of his pants or in his silk sleeves with a rubber band. Machine riders think they can get every ounce of run out of a horse.

Track authorities shake you down if they suspicion somebody's packing—you get suspended if you get caught. At the starting gate they make everyone dismount—pony riders, too. I wouldn't carry a machine for a jock when I ponied, but some pony people would. They'd smuggle it in and pass it to the jock at the last minute.

It's easy to tell if a horse is plugged in. When a horse gets shocked it swings its tail in a circle. We'd watch the replays and see a horse's tail suddenly swing around and say, Gee, I wonder what happened there?

It's a prominent thing at the cheaper tracks—or it used to be. This jock packs, that jock packs. You'd hear stories about the jock and his girlfriend—how he plugs her in when they're having sex.

GRANDSTANDING

If something strange happens, riders say, *Shit fire, save me some matches!* They sing little jingle ditty things. They holler, *Coming on the inside!* or *Whoa back!* Sometimes a horse'll throw his rider and come barreling at you when you're galloping during workouts. Then they yell, *Heads up! Loose horse!*

In the early morning when it's still dark with just a few lights up, you'll be galloping down the empty track and hear *thump, thump, thump, thump*—hoofbeats behind you. It's beautiful. And riders will stand straight up on their horses then—they call it grandstanding. They stand up and stretch out their arms and say, *Thought I was a coyote, but I'm all right now.*

BLACK SHOE POLISH

A jockey's horse spooked and broke through the outside fence into a line of trees. The jockey comes to in the hospital and the doctor asks, When was your last bowel movement? Right before I hit that first tree, the jockey says.

After a bad race, a trainer asks his jockey, What happened? And the jockey says, Well, once we hit the seven-eighths pole he started making weird noises. The trainer gets worried and says, What kind of noises? Was he bleeding, or wheezing, or what? The jock says, No, it was more like *oink oink*—he's a pig.

They call it breaking the maiden—the first time a jockey wins a race. When a jockey breaks his maiden, all the other jockeys come and strip him and put black shoe polish on his balls—did you know that?

6

EVERYTHING MYSELF

People took notice of my record with the Beauregards and started sending me horses to train. I didn't ever want a big stable because I didn't want to worry about hiring grooms and exercise riders— I wanted to do everything myself. So I'd train two or three—groom them and exercise them, too—and to make extra money I pulled manes, cleaned sheaths. I ponied other horses to the starting gate for twenty-five bucks a trip. I'd gallop them at eight bucks a pop.

The trainer figures out the horse's game plan, but the groom cleans the horse's stall, scrubs his feed tub, does his leg care, brushes him, keeps him happy. A groom knows the horse better than anybody, but the only groom you ever hear about is Will Harbut, groom to Man o' War. The two of them lived together, retired together, died a few weeks apart. They were buried side by side. It was a love affair.

There'll be ten grooms in a barn but your horse will nicker at you and nobody else. You talk to them and they listen. They respond. You're their caregiver. They want to make you happy.

WASHED, BATHED, GOOD CARE

Four o'clock feed, seven days a week. After that you tack them up and get them out on the track. They see the saddle go by and they're arching their heads and bobbing up and down. While the horses are out, the stalls get cleaned. Water buckets get scrubbed, feed tubs get scrubbed. You don't put feed in a dirty old tub. You scrub.

If it's hot you use a hose, but most days you heat up water for a warm bath with a natural sponge and shampoo when they're done running. You clean their sheath with castile soap if they're a gelding, or if they're a mare, you clean their little tits. You might put a light fishnetty fly sheet on them, but typically your nice big squirrel-cage fans will keep the flies away.

You have your bandages laundered, rolled up, ready. You have your sheet cotton and your hoof packing. You groom them and put on leg liniments, run bandages. You might freeze their legs with ice or put them in a turbulator with epsom salts. They love to stand with the warm whirlpool water up past their knees. If their shoulders are stiff, you rub salve on and wrap them in plastic and pin a wool blanket around their neck. Pretty soon the sweat starts dripping. It loosens them up, makes them feel good.

On race days, you sprinkle this green powder—it looks like dope—onto a little piece of sheet cotton and light it on fire under the horse's nose. There's belladonna in it, among other things. You put a bucket on the ground and drape the horse with a raincoat so he can really steam open his head. All this crap—snot, phlegm, mucus—pours from his nose into the bucket.

Once, some trainer's kids who hung around the track thought they'd be smart and smoke it, too. They smoked it, then ran around like squirrels.

YOU CHECK IT, YOU SHAKE IT

You got your triple-tie timothy hay bales, a hundred pounds each. Oats come in ninety-six-pound sacks. No one's going to run up and say, *Oh, Miss, let me get that for you!* You carry your own. You lift them.

No mold, no dust. A feed man with iffy thistle hay won't get through the track gates, but there could be a leak in your barn roof, so you check it, you shake it. With a heave-y horse you might have to soak the hay even if it don't seem dusty no more.

Some horses want a wet mash to eat—you put beet pulp and boiling water in their feed and mix it up. You check their stool and make adjustments. This one's a little loose. This one's hard like road apples—he needs more bran. A bleeder will get extra alfalfa for the K-C vitamins, which helps clot the blood.

Vets and farriers make their rounds. *Everything all right here? Need anything?* You might want to hang a jug on a horse. The vet'll give copper, iron, arsenic, strychnine, a B12 cocktail. A nervous horse you give thiamin, B1 — it takes the edge off. Others need electrolytes to help them bounce back after a race.

If a horse is bored or hurting, he'll paw a hole in the ground in his stall. You fill it with water because he won't like the splash, or you pack it with dirt and smooth it level and sprinkle a little hot red pepper on top.

Stall weavers can't keep weight on because of their nervous high metabolism, but you can put some water in a plastic milk jug and hang it up for them to bang on. They'll stand in front of their webbing and mess with that jug all day.

If a jug don't work you get them a goat or miniature pony — little mascots to keep them happy. The mascot lives in the stall with the horse and calms him right down.

A THOUSAND POUNDS
OF PRESSURE

Galloping, a horse spends a lot of his time suspended in the air—flying, really—or on one foot. When a foot lands, there's a thousand pounds of pressure held up by that one thin leg, that little hoof the size of a hand-held ashtray.

If a hoof breaks and you need to grow it out, you put Reducine on a toothbrush and rub, rub, rub it on the coronet band. It stimulates blood flow and pretty soon that band will swell. To keep the sole soft for growth, you stir up Bowie Clay with water, salt and vinegar in a bucket like a mud pie, then cut circles from heavy paper feed sacks and splat—you plop the mud on and pack the paper to the bottom of the hoof.

Before you shoe them, you x-ray each foot to see where those coffin bones lie. Some horses are low in the heel so they'll get wedges or mud nails or caulks or blocks. If they've got a long stride, they might overreach and grab their quarters and take a chunk out of their coronet. Then they're gouging blood all over.

A good trainer will go out and walk the track to check the surface before a race. It might be rubberized Tartan or it might be turf. Some dirt tracks have more sand, others have more clay. Track staff harrow after each race—you see them out there dragging. There shouldn't be no rocks. The surface has got to be smooth.

WE'RE HUNGRY!

On shipping day you haul the horses in a big trailer and when you arrive at the next track, you have to set up their stalls and get them taken care of right away. The horses can taste the difference in water from track to track, but if you put Coca-Cola in it—just a little, to sweeten it up—they'll be more tempted to drink. Then of course you have to wean them off the Coca-Cola because if they test positive for caffeine you'll be ruled out.

They get knocked off their feed easy, too. They get tired, they feel ill. They see that big tub of food and say, *This is too much—I can't even look at it.* They shit in their feed tub to send you the message.

You try things. Maybe give them just a little handful. Maybe feed the others first. You show up, you're barely awake, it's four o'clock, but they're all banging and boy—they're whinnying, *Good morning, here we are, we're hungry!* If there's one who's off his feed, you let him sit there and think about it. You let his mouth water, watching the others eat first.

It's like if you're fasting and nervous before blood work and you see a bunch of people munching on fresh cinnamon rolls and drinking coffee—suddenly you can't wait to get some, too. If you're sick to your stomach and somebody brings you a big tray of food, you say, *Get it out of here!* But if they bring you a half piece of dry toast or a little cup of soup, you think, *I can do this.* Gradually you get yourself back in your feed tub.

STRAIGHT OFF THE GOAT

At Deerheart, Nebraska, we all ran around in golf carts—from the backside of the barns up to the racing office, over to the kitchen and that. Bobbie Mackintosh milked Winnie the goat, who was a mascot for a racehorse called Springtime Notion. When she wasn't in her stall with Springtime, Winnie'd jump on Bobbie's golf cart and away they'd go.

I was having a terrible time with my stomach, and one day Bobbie heard me complaining about it. She said, Sonia, have some goat milk. She gave it to me straight off the goat—nasty, not pasteurized or nothing—but right away my stomach felt better, and then I was fine.

If you're sick, you wait for the veterinarians to come around and treat you, too. The jockeys got B12 shots before each race—three, four B12 shots a day. You'd say, Oh, I'm exhausted, and the vet'd give you a B12 shot. If you had a bad tooth you pulled it yourself.

Once I was up for five wins in a row with Miss Sotmoore—she was one of my best mares—but I had a fever and I could hardly move.

Another trainer said, If you want to come over, I'll have Mom give you a shot of—I don't know what it was. It might've been cattle antibiotics. This fellow happened to live about twelve miles from the track so I went home with him and bent over the kitchen sink and his mom gave me the shot. Within three hours I was a new person. I got to see my horse run, and we won our fifth in a row.

7

I KNOW WHAT I KNOW

Why is this horse backing up? Why is this horse not running like she used to? What happened here? The trainer watches the race replays again and again. The trainer has to figure it out. There's always puzzlers. Just when you think you know a lot about a horse he'll show you how stupid you really are.

You study the film to learn about the other horses, too. Some like to go to the front and they have enough staying power to close. Others like to come off the pace, come from behind. Some come on the inside. Some don't like to be on the rail.

The best trainers work with what the horse wants to do. You want to see them bounce off the track, swinging their tail. You want a happy horse at the front of its stall, popping its head up, talking to you, nickering, cleaning up its feed.

You watch their ears—are they perked, happy? Pinned back, pissed off? Look at their eyes. A dog can have pleading eyes, begging eyes—it wants a biscuit. You look at a horse's eyes—are they bright, alert? Or does it have a dull eye?

You see a horse at the back of its stall—that's not good. That horse is starting to get sour.

THEY GET THEIR HEADS JERKED OFF

It'll happen that an owner wants to see his horse run—don't matter there's no race written for him. He's in town for the weekend and wants to show off to his friends. So he pushes the trainer to put a horse worth two thousand in a race for eight. The horse is outclassed. It's going to get its head jerked off.

When a horse runs where he don't belong, he runs dead last. You do it often enough, he starts to feel like a loser. He gets depressed. He's sore and broke down because he's running so hard to keep up with the better horses. Pretty soon he develops a sour attitude and stops eating.

To build the horse's confidence back up, you pet him aggressively on the neck—*Oh, good boy!* You go overboard with the petting and hugging. He starts to think better of himself.

In morning workouts, you pick three companions and go head-to-head on the track at a gallop. When you give the signal, the other riders let you pull forward. It's like a fixed race. Your sour horse gets a burst of winning feeling. You do it again and again, and after a while, the horse gets his heart pumped back up.

I THINK YOU'LL BE SAD

Director Dean—he was fathered by Charlie Stut, Doctor Stut, a really good horse, an old class horse, a fifty, sixty thousand dollar horse.

Director Dean was owned by Hank Killdeer of Killdeer Ford in Chance Rapids. Hank Killdeer kept talking about selling Director Dean. I said, You don't want to sell him, he's going good.

Hank Killdeer says, I'm offered a good price for him.

Oh sure, I say. They seen him in the workouts. They seen him training like a bear. He's stake horse material.

Hank says, Are you sure he's good?

I say, He's very good.

Hank says, Well, it's kind of nice. It's a lot of money they're offering.

So I stick my neck out. I say, You do what you want, but come over tomorrow morning, I'll have Billy Fargo come. You take a look at him. I think you'll be sad if you sell him, I say.

So Hank Killdeer kept him. Director Dean ran third his first time. You need to give them a race just to get some air pumped into them—but he came in third. After that he ran out $130,000 as a two-year-old. He won the stakes.

Hank Killdeer says, I'm so glad. He says, I was ready to sell him for five thousand.

After that, Hank Killdeer of Killdeer Ford sold my dad a brand-new truck for five thousand dollars.

BOBBLE, BOBBLE

You spend hours and hours with a horse—you fall in love with them. They run their hearts out for you. You know when they're hurting.

Janet M—she'd run like a house on fire, but she was getting sorer and sorer. I told the owner, We need to blister her and give her some time, bring her back next spring.

Oh no, the owner says, she wants to race—she's better than ever.

You're not there in the morning when she can't even stand up, I said. So I refused. I said I wouldn't train her no more.

The owner—Tricky Ricky people called him—he found somebody else to do it. Next time Janet M ran I was there, watching the race. Bobble, bobble—she busted her leg clean off.

I found Tricky Ricky afterwards. I said, You call yourself a horseman?

YOU CAN'T BLAME A MAN

Bob Bozeman was an owner who'd been a jockey. He weighed maybe 120 pounds soaking wet. His wife Charlene was a big woman with blonde, fluffy, weird hair like a movie star's. They had two grown daughters and then they had a little gal, Bebe, who was an accident—Charlene got pregnant when she was forty-four years old. The squirt was spoiled, spoiled, spoiled. She was a little friend who'd help me sometimes with the horses.

Bob was a big gambler, a little shaky. I was happy because I had a good stable of his horses to train, but he'd always put the screws to me. When he drank he'd take on the largest person he could find. One night a bunch of us were at a table at Hungry's to celebrate a win. You grilled your own steaks at Hungry's—big old sirloins, huge slabs of Texas toast. Bob got drunk and said, I'll put my dick down the neck of this beer bottle. He was working on it when Charlene stood up and said, Bobby, put that little thing away. The waitress came over and we got kicked out of the restaurant.

At draw time, the owner had to be present, but Bob lived in Oklahoma, so he said, We'll fix that problem right now and put the horse in your name. Well, wasn't that fine and dandy—on paper, I was the owner. But then when we win a nice race, guess who paid the tax?

Bob'd come down for the races on Wednesdays and Saturdays. He'd rent a motel room for the week and the room would sit empty on days he drove back to Oklahoma. One week when I'd been sleeping in my truck he said, You might as well stay at the motel since it's paid for, and he gave me the key. But then he came back early and let himself into the room one night while I was asleep. He thought he'd get him some from me.

He was slick, tricky—a slippery son of a bitch. He pulled stunts that made me look like an idiot. You had to watch him. You had to learn. He respected it when you outsmarted him. You can't blame a man for trying, he'd say.

THIS HORSE, THIS RACE

His name was Dark Side. They had him on the kill truck for the slaughterhouse. When he was a baby, one of the brood mares kicked him in the head, knocked out one of his eyes. There was a big socket there, caved in but covered with fur, with a couple little eyelashes poking through.

He wasn't mine at the time but I'd been watching him awhile. Then one day somebody said, That horse you like so well is gonna be slaughtered.

I said to Bob Bozeman, We need to get this horse. We can buy him for kill price, eight hundred bucks. That's when kill price was high. Bob said, If you think you can do something with him, make us some money, I'll fund it.

The killer already had six other horses loaded—Dark Side was at the back. The killer said, You'll have to give me an extra hundred—I've got to unload all these others to get him. So Bob gave me an extra hundred and I gave it to the killer.

Dark Side had been ruled off for flipping in the gates. You can get a flipper reinstated, but it's a lot of work. You have to get reapproved by the starter and you have to have eight clean breaks.

Horses get fractious and bang around in their slots before you kick the latch, so they've got headers to hold them. Here's Dark Side, in a middle hole, with a handler on each side yanking his head straight. On his blind side there's stamping and whinnying, heavy bodies slamming on metal, but he can't turn his head to look because the headers won't let him. That's when he'd panic and start in with his fits.

Morning workouts are from five until eleven. There's a lot of traffic. I'd walk him, just halter and lead shank, up to the starting gates to take a look around. I'd pet him and talk to him. I talked to the gate crews. Did a long lot of talking to the starters and headers. I said, Don't crank him down like that. Let him turn his head a little and look.

Some of the other trainers would say, Get over it, the fucker's got one eye. You're wasting your time. They acted like cowboys. They liked me okay but I was still a girl trainer. Everything you do you've got to do twice as good.

I found an exercise rider, a good little jockey named Valdez — he took his time with him. We got some clean breaks. Finally the starter says, Okay, he's reapproved, you can run him — but one more quirk, the horse is off and there ain't no bringing him back.

I talked to my owner, Bob. I said, Let's run him next week. It's a race written for us, I said. So we entered, grabbed the seven hole. It was a lucky slot because it's a nine-horse field — he'd have just two on his blind side.

Dark Side goes off at twenty-five to one. That's a fifty-two-dollar winner. Bob said, Can I put some money down? Yes, I said, he's ready.

The horse seemed to know I spared him. Everyone had given up on him. I've trained expensive horses and I've trained cheaper ones, but this was one of the best moments—this horse, this race. It turned a lot of heads. I finally got recognition as a trainer.

Bob was very happy. He made a bundle of money on the gamble. He got the exacta, trifecta. We won another four or five races after that. But then Dark Side got crippled up—suspensories—and Bob sold him at the fall sale. I couldn't do a thing about it because he wasn't my horse. Bob always sold all his horses at the fall sale, then he'd start out fresh for spring.

Some other trainer bought him. He never won another race. Don't know if he flipped in the gates again but every time he seen me at the track he'd spin his head around and whinny.

8

RACETRACKERS

You're around some really prominent people and some are just as common as old shoes.

FANCY SUITS, FANCY BOOTS

Tim Tucker's parents were wealthy, and they bought him expensive racehorses to train. He wore fancy suits and fancy boots and dark sunglasses and after a few months on the scene he thought he knew everything. He did well, got several wins, but mostly because his horses were so expensive to begin with. All he had to do was drop them in.

Once, after his horse beat my horse, I said, Congratulations Tim, your horse ran a good race, and he said, Sonia, suck my dick.

The next day, my boss says to me, Sonia, do you know where those bute pills are? He'd just gotten a new bottle from Charblatt. I said, Maybe Tim borrowed them. I wasn't being nasty—that's what we did. We borrowed things, loaned things, helped each other out. But when my boss asked him, Tucker said, I didn't take them—but maybe that dumb cunt who works for you did.

I found Tucker and we had a brawl. He pulled my shirt way up and we were rolling around on the ground. My boss had to drag me off. Tucker was crying and the next day he had a black eye. Everybody was happy about it. They were really rubbing it in.

If you start a fistfight at the racetrack you're supposed to be banned a few months, but instead the stewards said, Sonia, what can we buy you for breakfast?

Tucker did change after that. And a few years later, when I was injured so bad I almost died, he's the one who invited me to stay with him and his wife in their trailer at the racetrack. When I got out of the hospital I couldn't even sit up on my own, but Tucker and his wife—they took good care of me.

PAUPER'S HILL

There was a fellow with long hair, an exercise rider, who got caught robbing a Dairy Queen. When they arrested him, he pulled out a penknife and cut himself with it. They took him to jail and he hung himself in his cell that night.

They found his racing license, but he was using a phony name. Cops came out to the racetrack to investigate the identity of this young man who'd committed suicide in the jail, but we had nothing to tell them.

A few weeks later we heard he was to be buried in a pauper's grave, so my friend and I went. I don't know why. We barely knew him. We paid respects. There was no tombstone, just a little plastic marker with his fake name, so my friend and I asked the cemetery if we could make our own stone for him. Back at the track, we laid boards down, poured cement, and set a horseshoe in each corner.

Pauper's Hill they called it. The pauper's part was really pretty. When our tombstone was dry, we took it out to his grave with some little flowers from the racetrack.

Later we saw an article about him. They'd finally found his true identity. He had warrants out for his arrest. His family decided to leave his body where it was.

THE OLD LADY

Hoser was a hot walker who'd get drunk and start feeling people up. You never knew who he was trying to take home. He was after this young gal once, Lily, but she didn't like him. Lily's grandmother owned some horses and Lily would drive up to help her on weekends. The grandmother had a trailer in the park with the rest of us and when Lily came, the old lady would go back to where she was from and Lily would stay in the trailer.

One night when Hoser was lit up, he sneaked into the trailer where Lily was sleeping. He took his clothes off and crawled under the covers with her. But it wasn't Lily in the bed—it was the old lady. She was a tough old lady with bow legs and a big gruff voice, and she sat up and yelled, What in the hell?

Hoser screamed and ran out. He woke everybody up. We watched him run naked through camp, looking for his clothes. He forgot he'd left them in the old lady's trailer.

JAKE THE PRINCE

Jimmie was so skinny. He walked with a limp and his teeth were messed up. He was meek and mild and when he talked he was shy—a real nervous actor—and he had a little stutter. Anytime it rained he'd go out and dance in it. He had an old red pickup, a Dodge Ram, and he was always polishing the chrome ram on the hood with his T-shirt until someone stole it one day when he went into town.

Jimmie groomed a horse called Jake the Prince—a beautiful gray thoroughbred, a stakes-race winner, an unbelievable horse. Jimmie slept in tack rooms and took his footlocker track to track, traveling the circuit with Jake the Prince. Any chance Jimmie got he'd take Jake out to graze. He'd lie on the ground while Jake ate grass and talk to him, pet him, give him apples. Jimmie and Jake were meant for each other. The horse would always nicker at Jimmie when he saw him coming.

Jimmie would say, Sonia, you want a candy bar? Sonia, you want some coffee? Oh sure, Jimmie, I'd say, that would be nice.

Sometimes we'd get tacos together at Ron Hegel's restaurant in Omaha, Nebraska. Everyone else thought he was weird—Crazy Jimmie! But he had the same boss for years and he was an excellent worker.

Jake the Prince ended up breaking a leg in a race and had to be put down. After that, nobody seen Jimmie for a while. We were worried about him. He wasn't a drunk by no means, but after he lost Jake, he went on a bender and disappeared for a month.

Eventually he came back and we went to Ron Hegel's for lunch one afternoon. After we ordered, Jimmie started talking and didn't stop. He told me about how he'd been a prisoner of war in Vietnam. He told it like he was reliving it. It was horrible, what he told me.

Back at the track, he showed me a folded piece of paper he kept in his footlocker. It was an article about when he and the other POWs got rescued. It listed the names of the soldiers and how long they'd been held. Jimmie was in there longest.

After his release, the army delivered all the letters he'd missed over the years. He found out his brother committed suicide and his mother died, too. He had nobody left when he came home.

I said, Jimmie, let's get you some benefits—you should be entitled to something, you deserve it. But he didn't want no one else to know about it. He was ashamed—or I don't know what he was—but he refused. He wanted nothing to do with the government—no money, no help, no way.

C'MON, CHARLIE!

Johnny Block kept a pet fox called Roxy, a badger called Red, a pheasant called Ted, some ferrets, a few snakes, a myna bird, and a crow called Charlie. Crows are great talkers and Charlie talked beautifully.

C'mon Charlie! Johnny would say, and Charlie would flap over and land on Johnny's shoulder. Charlie's wings were clipped to keep him from flying too far. At lunchtime he'd sit next to me and I'd share my sandwich with him. I'd toss the meat in the air and he'd catch it.

When I did chores in the stable, Charlie hopped from beam to beam above me and said, Hello, Hello! One of my racehorses then was a nice big horse called Three Tabs, over sixteen hands tall. Charlie liked to dive down and nail the horse's huge ears.

Then Charlie's wings grew out a little and one day he took off. Johnny called and called. Charlie, Charlie! Nothing. No Charlie. On the second day we were getting worried about Charlie.

There was a big tree behind the barn, not far from the shed row. That afternoon, the tree was full of crows. Johnny ran up to the tree and shouted, Charlie, Charlie! The birds took off in a flock — except one. Hello! Hello! said the bird. Come here, Charlie! Johnny said. He had to clip Charlie's wings again after that.

THE BIG DRINK

His name was Mick but we called him Humpty Dumpty. He was from Louisiana. When he went home for Christmas he'd bring back a bag of chicory coffee for me. He had a fat bald head, a big middle, little short legs. He was funny and jolly. He'd put his hands on his hips and cock his belly out and say silly stuff to make us laugh. He looked like a clown but he was a great horseman.

One night in January, a bunch of us went to a bar. We were working at a track in Michigan. After we finished our food, Mick said, I'm gonna go start the old gal up, and he went out to defrost his truck. He left it running while he settled his tab. But when he went out again to leave, the truck was gone. Next day, police found it wrecked in the river. Mick said, She took the big drink!

A few weeks later, after watering off for the night, I was driving from the track back to the room I'd rented in town. In Michigan it was so cold the water buckets froze — you had to hammer them out four, five times a day. I had a little topper on my truck and when the weather was warm I'd sleep back there. A mile down the road, someone knocked on the window behind my head. I almost crashed. I thought it was a man who wanted to murder me but it was Mick playing a trick.

WHERE'S THORBY?

A lot of my friends have gotten killed. A lot of them have steel rods down their spines. One guy lost his leg. He was a jockey who'd lost his leg, but he'd still gallop horses and pony them to the gate. Sometimes his fake leg would fall off when he was riding and someone had to run out and pick it up for him.

There's a lot of pain and pill abuse. You learn some of them are drunks. They show up to hot walk and they're drunk. When they say they're hungry, you don't give them money. You take them to get a bite instead.

The leg paint I used on the horses had alcohol in it. One morning I came in at four and said, Where's Thorby?

I finally found him passed out in an empty stall. I thought he was dead. He'd gotten into my tack box and drunk up all of my leg paint.

If you had a wild one, you gave it to Thorby—he'd jump on and hoot and holler. It was like he was glued to the horse.

He wouldn't ever fall off. Horses responded to him. Thorby was gentle but when he got drunk he'd pick a fight with a cigarette machine or a jukebox.

MIRACLE PERSON

My friend Bobbie Mackintosh was galloping a three-year-old and the three-year-old spooked. Bobbie's foot got tangled in the irons and she got dragged. Her neck broke—a hangman's break. She'd just gotten married the week before.

They life-flighted her off the racetrack and took her to the hospital. She was in a coma four months. She had a brain injury. When she woke up she was paralyzed except for her arms. She had to learn how to talk again. The husband dumped her, of course. He dumped her right away.

She got hurt in January. In late November, she showed up at the racetrack in a wheelchair. They let her work the pari-mutuel window. She talked real slow, but she remembered me. We used to hitch a ride to the racetrack together every morning at four back when we were staying at the El Rancho Motel—her and her boyfriend and me and the idiot I was with. She was the one who'd given me goat milk when I was sick. I knew her quite well.

Bobbie had to have surgeries all the time, and she was in therapy the rest of her life. She got a medical support dog and she got remarried, too. She was always working on her arm strength. You can read about her on the internet. Her doctors wrote testimonials about her determination and how she made history. She was known as a miracle person.

She just passed away last year. She wanted to write a book about her life. Anyway, she was from Minnesota.

HE WAS LIVING HIGH

There was a jockey I dated—Tommy Blue—a good jockey, a leading rider, a crazy little Cajun. He liked to eat at Preston's, a fancy steakhouse. He got to be good friends with the owner. Whenever Tommy came in the owner'd set him up with lobster and steak, the works, and Tommy would eat and eat and gorge himself. Then he'd throw it all up to maintain his weight.

The owner started asking Tommy things like, Got any live mounts tomorrow? And Tommy would say, Sure, I think I got a good chance in that race. Sort of innocent, in the beginning. Sort of polite, if anything. But then Tommy started gambling a little and next thing you know, he's getting introduced to big rollers, he's making promises, giving them tips, dirty stuff, getting money in return. He was living high, buying tailor-made suits and such— he was so small.

Sooner or later things go wrong—some dark horse comes in and beats you—and people are not happy. Suddenly Tommy had a lot of debt. He had people following him.

After I got back from Kentucky I went to visit him—we were still good friends. He told me he was going to kill himself and he described how he'd do it. I said we should go to a doctor. No, babe, I'm just kidding, he said. I would never, he said. Are you sure? I said. Of course, he said. Come on.

A week later I heard he'd done it. He'd told me what he was going to do, and he did it—to the letter.

I DIDN'T WANT NO DRAMA

Steve Silver is in the racing hall of fame, but when he drank he'd beat me. I was with him seven years. He wouldn't let me go.

You work at a racetrack, you get black eyes, bruised, cut up, knocked around—it's common. Maybe people suspected something but nobody asked. I didn't want no drama. But then one night some friends talked me into going to the bar with them and some other racetrackers. Steve Silver showed up and started raising Cain with me, making a big scene. My friends wouldn't tolerate it. They put him in the hospital. After that I finally got away.

Now I'm friends with his son Trevor. For a few years, Trevor lived with us in the summer when he was out of school. We stayed in Steve's little fishing cabin by a lake, not far from the track.

At first I hated the idea. I didn't particularly care for kids. I didn't want to be his mother. But he helped me with my horses —I paid him for it, he worked, he earned it—and we ended up best friends.

After his stupid dad died, we got reconnected. Trevor always says, You saved me—you saved me from drowning. I don't know if I saved him or not. All I did was go into the water and bring him back to shore with me.

9

THE RODEO STUNT

Old Cal Cantor's legs were bowed like he had a horse under him. When he came to the track I'd go to Dairy Queen with his wife and daughter. Cantor worked with rodeo stock, some of the best. His eldest son Donnie was a champion bull rider, third in the world. Connie Cantor, his younger one, was a bulldogger. Connie got gored by a bull, got his eye knocked out and his face was—I don't know how many reconstructions they did.

Cal Cantor said, Sonia, I've seen you with the horses, I want to hire you. I was getting tired of the track, so I went and worked on his ranch in South Dakota. It was next to a reservation, flat land all around. I could see why their boys were rodeo stars— those horses were like mustangs. You had to hobble them just to trim their feet. They'd never been touched, yet Cantor expected me to break them. He had me working construction, things I never knew nothing about. He had me sandblasting a metal starting gate in a lightning storm.

I worked with an Indian, Roger. He had a busted back but Cantor worked the hell out of him, this hardworking Indian. Cantor raised cattle and wheat, and he'd put Roger on his bumpy tractor and work him all day long. Roger lived on the reservation. On payday his relatives would come and try to collect his paycheck because he was one of the only people on the reservation with a job.

I worked with Harry Trulock, too. He was a quarter-horse jockey from Oklahoma. Cantor had miles and miles of land—corrals out in the middle of nowhere. One of Harry's jobs was to drive the cattle from corral to corral.

Harry liked to drink, so one day when he didn't come back from the range, everyone figured he'd gone on a bender.

While I was pulling fence the next day, I looked up and thought, What's this, a deer?

Here comes Harry Trulock, parched, lips cracked, skin burnt bright red. He'd gotten lost. All them acres, everything flat and crazy—all you see is power lines. Harry could hardly slide off his horse. We had to carry him inside. I don't know how he made it back.

HUNTERS AND JUMPERS

Dale and Chester Treska came to the fall horse sale every year in their monogrammed shirts and fancy streamlined vans to pick up prospects for their hunters and jumpers enterprise. They were always complimenting me, saying, Sonia, you need to get off the track, come work with us, so when I left Cantor's ranch I bought a bus ticket to Wilton, Wisconsin, but when I changed buses my luggage got lost. That was a sign. There I was—mucking stalls in Wisconsin in my nice clothes because I didn't have anything else.

Treskas liked horses with bad racing records. If a racehorse is sound, it can't run hard enough to hurt itself. If a horse can't run hard it's no good to us racetrackers. We always hoped the hunter and jumper people would get them so they'd have a better life.

Treskas would buy a racehorse for eight hundred bucks, teach him to go over a few jumps, then sell him six weeks later for eight thousand. Bracing Bill—they got ten grand for him.

They had the big name, the perfect setup. Wealthy families came to them for horses and for riding lessons, too—little rich kids at thirty-five dollars an hour. The rich people would be so happy—they'd say, Wow, my daughter's an equestrian! But Treskas didn't put none of that money in my pocket. I was working for room and board, living in their house. They treated me like a servant. I lasted two and a half months.

They liked to badmouth racetrack people, say what a bunch of crooks we were, but their horses would get crippled up and Treskas would hop and block them worse than racetrackers ever did.

10

I WAS GIVEN A CHOICE

A few months later I was back at the track, riding a horse to the gate for a race. Another horse bolted with the jockey on it and T-boned the horse I was on. The collision sounded like a shotgun blast. We all went down. I was at the bottom of the pile.

It happened in front of the grandstands. The crowd was traumatized. The medics did CPR, they used the shockers. It was a death experience.

They brought me back, but I was in a coma. I could hear every word but I couldn't respond. Racetrackers were coming in and out, talking with the doctors and nurses — Is she going to make it? They say your hearing's the last to go. I thought they would bury me alive.

I was given a choice to live or die. When I decided to live, I woke up. Then I was in a lot of pain. I had a lot of injuries, a lot of internal bleeding. I had all but two ribs broken, a punctured lung. I couldn't breathe, I couldn't walk.

Later, when the hospital sent me home, my racetrack family had to feed me and help me because I couldn't sit up on my own. I was renting a trailer in a court not far from the track, but I stayed next door with Tim Tucker and his wife for the first few weeks. They took good care of me—the Tuckers and some of the other guys' wives, too. They'd wheel me out to the track so I could talk to people and get some sun. One time they took me to a zoo.

THEY'D RATHER HAVE THE PISS

Healing up, I hung around the racetrack. You're not supposed to work in the test barns if you're a stable hand because you might be inclined to let the horse's piss run on the ground so they'd have to draw blood instead. Some drugs will show up in urine but not in blood—they'd rather have the piss. But they made a spot for me so I could earn a little bit of money. I had nothing coming in while I was in the hospital, and all the money I'd saved up—which was quite a chunk—it didn't take long to deplete it.

I was home for a week at Christmas when a friend from the Nebraska circuit called me. He'd heard I got hurt and said, You need to come down to Florida and winter up here, work for JR Boyd and Ransom Farms. This was a chance to be with the big-time horses, the big-time trainers. JR Boyd paid for my plane ticket and I went.

I was hired as a groom. I got every other afternoon off. Oh! the horses were so sound! I rubbed a horse worth five million. No need to whirlpool them or ice them or freeze them or run bandages. It was so easy. If a horse is in bad shape, the owner gives him the time he needs to rest, and if a horse's racing days get cut short, the owner makes his bundle on the horse's sexual services instead.

STOP MY WORLD, LADY!

There was a lot of wealth. The owner of the Yankees was our neighbor. I met a lot of famous people. Some of the wealthy owners were common, down-to-earth, but some strutted around in their hats. The trainers didn't wear blue jeans. The trainers wore suits. It was elaborate.

If a horse takes a dump in his stall, the groom immediately goes in and gets it out. It's not tolerable to a trainer or owner to walk by and see their horse standing in a pile of shit. You can't use a pitchfork near the animals—they're too valuable to risk it—so you take the horse out of his stall, then go in and get the piles.

When you put straw down you pack it, you pack it—it's got to be perfect. You beat the stalls until you can bounce a quarter off the bales. Mrs. Milkie was a richie-rich and one day after I'd put her horse away with a fresh bed, I heard her saying, Oh my god, oh my god!

I run over there and JR Boyd runs over there, too. We said, What's wrong? What happened? And she said, There's a piece of straw in Percival's tail!

STUPID CAMERAS, BIG LIGHTS

A local news channel sent a crew to the farm every few weeks. We'd bring a horse out and parade him around and say who he's out of and who he's by, grandson of so-and-so, and the horse'd be nervous because the newspeople were idiots with their cords and microphones and their stupid cameras and big lights that blinded the animal.

There was a horse I introduced as Hell Mountain, but after the newspeople left, some trainers came up to me and said, Who's Hell Mountain? Where'd you get that? That ain't right.

Down there they don't say, What's his name? They say, What his name is? The accent is thick. So I'd asked, What his name is? But instead of H-A-I-L, I heard H-E-L-L.

There was a lot of drugs in Florida. We were all getting ready for the trip to Kentucky for the Derby in the spring. Workers at the farm would buy cocaine to sell in Louisville, Lexington. There was all these money scams, illegal schemes. It's how a lot of people got by.

GRAB THAT THING

JR Boyd was a five-time Indy 500 winner. His son did the training, but it was the old man, the race-car driver, who'd invested the money and started the farm. Both were named JR Boyd and there was the little one they called Hemorrhoid, the grandson.

One day a greenhorn gal came around asking for a job. She didn't know much about horses but she loved them and thought they were beautiful—she'd taken riding classes as a kid. Between spits of tobacco, Old Boyd said, These ain't riding horses. But the gal was pretty so he hired her as a hot walker.

When you walk them you've got to put a chain over their nose and under their lip to keep pressure on it and jingle it—the gal was struggling. Old Boyd was watching her. Then he said, See that horse over there? He pointed to a stallion, a little two-year-old, with its dick hanging out. The stallion kept slamming his dick up to his belly and bringing it down again.

Boyd said, The horse can't run like that, he's got his mind on other things. You've got to take care of him. Go grab that thing, you know how to do it. Is that a problem for you?

Well, no, said the greenhorn gal.

She touched the horse's dick and it jerked up—thump!—on his belly. She tried to grab it and it swung up and hit his belly again. Her hand went back. Oh my god, she said.

Boyd was waving his arm in the air, shouting for everyone to gather around—come on, come see this gal, get over here and take a look at this.

MILLIONS

When we hauled the horses from the training farm in Florida to Kentucky, I rode in the trailer with them to make sure nothing happened. It was a thirteen, fourteen hour trip. No seat belt—no seat, even—for me back there, but the rules get bent when you're hauling millions of dollars in horseflesh. Every time a horse took a munch of hay, the wind whipped the hay into my eyes—I had to wear sunglasses. If I needed something I was out of luck. When we stopped to gas up I'd get out and stretch.

Finally we arrived. Ransom Farm was beautiful—everything manicured. A huge crew worked seven days a week to maintain the grounds—polishing, clipping, raking, sweeping. There were people who did nothing but dust the stalls. There was a cemetery for the horses with life-size bronze statues on the graves. The barn roofs were all inlaid cedar. At the entrance were the big old iron gates that opened up to let you in, if you were lucky.

IT WAS HARD LIVING

It was the good horses and the big races and the twin spires at Churchill Downs. I thought, This is the Kentucky Derby and I'm here—this is my dream. I started from the bottom and worked my way to the top. But I didn't have a position like I did at the cheaper tracks—I was working as a groom, not a trainer.

In Kentucky there were dormitories for backsiders but if you lived there you had to follow their rules—no visitors, lights out at ten. I had a lot of friends and I liked to sit around and bullshit by the training track, so instead I lived in a horse stall with a concrete floor. It had a little wall heater, bars on the windows, a big heavy-duty metal door, one outlet. I lived out of a hot pot, an air bed. It would've been better if I'd had a car. I should've gotten a car.

The work was easier, the horses were healthier, the tracks were gorgeous. There was even a bus for backsiders—it'd take you to the local mall on your afternoons off. I suddenly had a lot of free time. Never had that in the leaky roof circuit. But my successes as a trainer and exercise rider were greater at those cheaper tracks. I started to think, Wow—this is it? This is terrible. I don't want to do it no more.

I TRIED TO BE A
NORMAL PERSON

For years and years you're around nobody but racetrack people. You don't have time for family. Your romantic relationships are short-lived because a rolling stone catches no moss. It's hard, it's grueling, it's up and down. I had a lot of injuries. I could've been paralyzed real easy. The doctors stressed that to me — it wouldn't take much.

I missed my folks. They were getting older. My dad had diabetes, and then my mom got diagnosed with colorectal cancer. My sister was in a mental institution — she couldn't help.

I suppose I was satisfied with what I'd done. My parents sacrificed a lot for me. It felt like it was time I did something for them. So I moved home and tried to be a normal person. I got a job at a factory.

Nice people I was working with, nice hours. Regular paycheck — it just wasn't very big and there was no chance of improving it. It was a smaller-scale business, family-owned. They paid what they could pay.

I had Rowdy still, and then I got Mick, a quarter horse off the Turnpike Ranch in Montana. I didn't stop with horses after I left the track—it was just different. I had my horses for pleasure. Keith Baxter was gone—lung cancer—so I boarded them at Bruce Wexford's stable. Bruce was in his eighties, half-Indian, fit as a fiddle—a cool old cowboy, an ex-rodeo rider. He was my friend.

After I'd been home a few months, I got a job offer from a top-notch breeding farm in Florida—but how boring. The same old horses, the same old faces, day after day, month after month. At the track it was hundreds of people, hundreds of horses. I turned it down. I clocked in to my shift at nine the next morning and clocked out again at five.

THE HORSE TAUGHT ME
ABOUT LIFE

I got another year with Rowdy after I came home. He was thirty-five when he died. Even dying, he was stubborn. He wanted to live. I was sitting on the ground next to him with my hands on his side. We were together twenty-eight years.

I had a friend who could talk to animals, and one day he came out to the stable to see me. I was sitting in the pasture with Rowdy while he grazed. My friend told me to walk away, then he said something in Rowdy's ear. After that, Rowdy started following me like a dog.

He never does that, I said. What did you say to him?

I asked him if he loves you, my friend said.

A few months after Rowdy passed, Bruce Wexford brought home a little mustang he'd bought from a rodeo sale in Minnesota. Chico was in such bad shape we had to have a petition about whether he could live at the stable. He'd just gotten out of quarantine in Mexico, and then he got the strangles. He was skin and bones and really scarred up—tattooed all over.

I ended up buying him from Bruce. I worked with him when I wasn't at the factory. I got some weight on him, some calm.

11

MISTER BAKER

Pretty soon I met a guy and he seemed all right. I thought he was great because he liked to camp, he liked the outdoors. I moved out of my folks' house and rented a little apartment with him. But then he started acting weirder and weirder, and when I'd had enough I told him I was leaving. It's not over until I say it's over, he told me, and the next day he tried to kill me in the tack room at Bruce's stable.

He came up behind me while I was cleaning Chico's bridle. He knocked me down, sat on my chest, put a rope around my neck. He squeezed it tighter and tighter and when I'd almost blacked out, he loosened up and let me breathe a little. He was always talking about how much he missed his mother—she died when he was a kid. I was gurgling blood but I said, Your mom, what would she think? That snapped him out of it. He dropped the rope, jumped on his bike, took off.

I was still lying on the ground when Bruce came wheeling in. My eyes were red and I had rope marks on my neck, bruises starting. Bruce said, What in the hell?

At the police station they took pictures of my injuries. I gave them the guy's name, his description. They found him that afternoon and put him in jail. But at the factory the next day, a woman from the police department called on my lunch hour. This is just to let you know that Mr. Baker—*Mister* Baker—has been released, she said.

After that I couldn't go to the stable unless Bruce was there with his shotgun. His hands shook like crazy but he stood by with his gun ready while I took care of Chico and Mick. At home, my dad kept a loaded revolver next to his chair in the den. He had baseball bats propped in the other rooms.

Then one day I found my favorite tabby cat hung by a noose at the barn. Bruce said, He'll kill your horses next. I was watching Mick and Chico graze in the pasture when suddenly Chico reared up and started striking the air, and I saw Baker out there crawling on his hands and knees like a dog.

I ran to the barn phone and called the police. The sheriff's department arrived and all of us went out to the muddy field to look. Bruce said, Here's a toe print, and here's the knee print. Looks like he's gone now, said the sheriff.

Nearby was an empty grain wagon with a ladder on the side. One of the deputies started climbing it, but when he got halfway up, Baker jumped out the top, swinging a little hatchet. He ran into a ravine behind Bruce's barn. The deputies didn't shoot. An officer gave Bruce a nightstick and they went into the swampy woods together, but Baker was gone.

All night I listened to the police scanner. They seen Baker by the bridge, they seen him by the school. Then he disappeared.

They found out he'd escaped from federal prison—they thought he'd drowned. I was escorted to and from work every day. I had to change my hours to accommodate the patrolmen's schedule. I had to move my horses to Waterfield, twenty miles away. I couldn't go out and enjoy myself. I was always looking over my shoulder. It wore my parents down—I could see it in their faces.

Well, guess what? I started going to college. I went into law enforcement. I thought, My rights have been violated. I'm going to find out how the system works. I'm not going to run.

THIS SUCKER

I studied law enforcement part-time. Did quite well, got all As and Bs. I paid my way working full-time at the factory. I was forty, forty-one years old.

I did an internship at a halfway house for people just out of prison. I wanted to go right up among them because I thought they were like him. I wanted to get in their heads. But they were mostly poor people with drug problems.

The lady at the halfway house said, Sonia, why don't you work in a prison? I worked in a prison, she said, state penitentiary —good pay, better than a cop, just think of it. You take some tests— you have to get a certain percentage. The session's only four or five hours long, she said, and if you pass, you can get a job as a correctional officer.

I thought, Sounds good to me. Maybe one day this sucker will walk through the prison doors and there I'll be. I'll say, What took you so long?

WITH THE MEN

Two prisons called me for an interview—Jasper City, a women's prison, and Onakona State Penitentiary, with the men.

At Jasper City, the warden asked me questions at a long table in a big room. She said she'd let me know. Then, at Onakona, they hired me on the spot. I did the drug test, piss test, blood test. I went to their academy where a lot of information was given. I got my certificate and went to work.

I'd respond to codes, take down my fair share. I'd get right in the middle of a knife fight. I done it. I did all right. I was fit and strong. Sometimes I could get more done, being a woman.

Not many females working at a maximum, so the inmates— you can't blame them. Sexual misconduct, flashing their dicks. You write them up, you ignore it. I'd worked at the racetrack all those years. I was used to it.

I had to watch them in the showers, stark ass naked. I didn't gloat in it. They put you there. You did what you had to do.

I didn't get embarrassed, or if I did, I didn't show it.

LA VEDETTE

You see some really tough stuff. You see all kinds of nonhuman behavior. After a while it makes you a different person. It makes you kind of cold.

There was a lot of dirty staff—harder than the inmates. There were officers who did sadistic things to their wives and kids. There were prisoners serving twenty years for a marijuana cigarette, yet officers would smoke dope in the parking lot on their lunch break.

You see the prisoners who get preyed on continuously—the little guys, the ones with mental problems. The officers don't care if they take their meds or not. They like to let them go around paranoid, scared to death. You see the inmates try to hang themselves. Some did hang themselves.

Somebody gets raped on a stairwell or strong-armed out of the money his family sent him—no one cares. Everything's a hustle, a hustle, a hustle. You see a lot, and some of it stays with you.

There was an inmate whose wife and kids got killed on Christmas. They were driving back to La Vedette after visiting him. There was ice on the roads and they died in a car crash on the highway.

I had to pull the inmate out of his cell and take him to the chaplain that night to break the news. At first the inmate assumed it was his grandfather who'd passed.

I thought, I wish it was your grandfather instead. I'm so sorry, I said.

The next day I got called in. My supervisor wanted to know: Are you a bleeding heart for these convicts?

HER BLACK MOUSTACHE

The higher-ups would always say, Never believe a convict. But as soon as an inmate says to another inmate, She likes me, or, She smiled at me, they have to investigate. They were constantly investigating me.

It wasn't unfounded. Some of the female officers, nurses, counselors—they fall in love. It happens. But just as often there'd be relationships between inmates and male officers, yet the male officers never got investigated. No one talked about it.

The more you make, the lazier you get. Some of the officers sat around and played cards while I did their jobs for them. I'd find shanks, hooch. Then they'd harass me because I made them look bad.

I broke up a fight once. I had the guy on the ground in hand-cuffs before anyone else showed up. The captain said, Nice job, but don't let it go to your head. He said, You women are only here because the state mandates it.

Onakona Penitentiary is huge, dark, old—it looks like a castle. It's made of stone cut from cliffs by the river. The first prisoners quarried the rock, carried it, stacked it up, walled themselves in.

For a while they kept women there, too. One gal escaped—she was serving thirty years for poisoning her husband. She made a man's coat and pants from the wool she was in charge of sewing for inmates' uniforms. She was seen by some meandering up the main street of town—casually twirling her black moustache—before she disappeared.

BLONDE, CUTE, BIG DIMPLES

Years go by. Then, one day in early spring, a farmer was moving his cattle from a field and stumbled over what was left of Baker. Finally I got some peace because they found his stinking remains.

The field where they found him was behind Bruce's stable. They said his heart exploded. He'd been waiting for me to come back.

At first they thought the body might've been Kellie Lankershim, the local news anchor who'd been missing for years.

That bitch reminds me of my old girlfriend, Baker would say when we watched the six o'clock news. He kept a picture of the girlfriend in his wallet and showed it to me once. She did look a lot like Kellie Lankershim—blonde, cute, big dimples.

Kellie disappeared the week after Baker strangled me at the stable. Guess what? Her apartment was in a complex by the river where one of Baker's doper friends lived. Baker's doper friend had a white van. The morning Kellie disappeared, someone saw a white van peeling out of the parking lot where Kellie's purse and keys were found.

When I heard that, I went to the police station and told them what I knew. But they didn't listen to me and they never found her.

For a while I went on search parties for Kellie Lankershim. We searched the fields and woods. I talked to Kellie's sister and mother. I tried to do something.

12

ONAKONA

Working at the prison, I got to where I didn't like myself anymore, so I quit. But it's where I met Jerry. He was a correctional officer, too. He quit a few years after I did. We started going to flea markets and got friendly with some of the dealers. They'd say, You two ought to set up a booth. That's what we do now—travel around on weekends, sell things.

We stayed in Onakona. We bought a little house in the country on top of a hill. We can look for miles from our front porch. We see eagles and deer and hear coyotes at night. There's a cute main street downtown and the beautiful Mahaskah State Park.

The American Gothic painter was born in Onakona and he's buried here, too. He was gay, married to a woman. When they divorced, the painter's family disowned him. The painter didn't want to be buried with his family but he ended up in their plot anyway, under their big stone lion. His tombstone is just a little square with his name and years. He didn't want nothing fancy.

Later they named the local school for him. There's an annual art festival in his honor. He grew up in a house not far from mine. They say he painted on rocks there and if you're lucky you'll find one.

I kept Chico and Mick at a stable nearby for awhile. They'd graze in the same big pasture this painter used to sit in with his easel and canvas and his little folding stool. The pasture looks like his paintings—hilly, rolling, really green. At one end of the field is a falling-down barn with one of the painter's murals on it, but nobody did anything to preserve it and you can hardly see it now.

BAD WEATHER OR NOT

Last year my dad passed away and my mom came and lived with us with her cancer. I had her for all those years, with her other cancer. She passed away May 13th, the day after Mother's Day.

When I left home for the track, I couldn't take Rowdy with me—I kept him at Baxter's where he got the basic care he needed. Year after year, my mom would drive to the stable a few times a week to brush him and talk to him. Used to be she didn't drive in winter—she'd take the bus to work when it snowed—but she drove out to see Rowdy bad weather or not.

She'd take him for walks and bring him treats. He had a nice barn, a nice stall, a heated water bucket. As he got older he got to stay in at night and during the day, too, if it was cold. After a while he had to have hot bran mashes a few times a week and some highfalutin vitamins. When his joints got arthritic I'd mail bute pills and my mom would crush them with a coffee bean grinder and mix them with pancake syrup and put it in a big oral syringe she'd squirt into the side of his mouth.

When I was a kid I had birthday parties for Rowdy, and after I left my mom had them for me. She'd take pictures of him and mail them to me at the track. He'd have a birthday hat on, a spread of gingersnaps and molasses cookies and cupcakes in front of him, frosting on his muzzle.

My mom would be having a bad day, a stressful week, but once she was with Rowdy, she felt better. Rowdy and I have lots of secrets, she'd say.

IT AIN'T LIKE A CAT

Chico and Mick both passed a few years ago. I don't have horses now. We're always doctoring because of Jerry's health, and I had some things going on, too. We're away on weekends at sales. It ain't like a cat where you put a sandbox out, a little dish of food and water. If you have a horse you've got to be there.

Back when kill price was high, a horse was worth more than a cow, per pound—people were raising them on feedlots for slaughter. Then the big kill plant in Texas closed, and prices went down to nothing. Suddenly there was free horses everywhere—the internet was full of them. My phone was ringing off the wall with people trying to give them to me. But there ain't no such thing as a free horse.

They say horse racing is cruel, but there's more cases of cruelty with backyard stable people. No one knows anything about hoof care, teeth floating. They think they can turn a horse out on grass, but when there's no grass the horse starves to death.

Some neighbors of mine were feeding theirs bread from the bread truck. When one horse died, I called the state. In the meantime the others died of malnourishment, too. It took three horses lying there dead—rotting, and me calling and calling—before someone finally came to investigate, but there was no fine, no consequence.

PERENNIALS

This week I've been busy, but I've got to get those pictures of Rowdy in the mail for you. My cousins have been here and I was shampooing carpets before that.

It did snow once. We had a light dusting last week. It's too early for it. We didn't have time to bring the flowers in or mulch the beds. My potted plants froze. I threw a coat over one big rosemary, but the others died. Of course some of the perennials will survive even if they're not properly zoned for this area. Today it's supposed to be sixty degrees.

The Amish put rubberized fabric between the rows to keep the weeds down, but I didn't do that this year and I lost a lot of strawberries. We might build raised beds next spring.

Last night Jerry and I watched a criminal show about JR Boyd and Ransom Farms. The big man at Ransom when I was there was JR Boyd's friend, BJ Bundy. The two of them liked to hop on their jet and take it wherever they wanted. They were spending lavishly and Bundy was mismanaging the farm—he borrowed more and more.

Galewood was their most valuable horse, but then he died under mysterious circumstances and everything fell apart. Ransom went under. Everyone thought Bundy killed Galewood for the insurance payout, but nothing was ever proved.

REMEMBER THIS?

There was a big racetrackers' reunion recently at Horsemen's Park. I wanted to go, but if you go, you end up wanting to go back to the track. People say you never get racing out of your blood. I still dream about it most nights.

I've got my Nebraska bunch. I've got my Florida and Kentucky friends, too. Someone'll say, Hey, remember so-and-so? They're usually talking about a horse but sometimes it's a person.

Rod Greer, he's been at it forty-five years. There's jockeys who aren't jockeys anymore but they still gallop horses. There's grooms who've taken a little time off and then gone back to the track. Trainers still own racehorses but now they hire someone else to do the training. Some have sons or daughters in the business. A few of the stallions I took care of still sire offspring. Those foals are running in races today.

By the time you're my age you've had a lot of injuries. And where there's injuries, you get arthritis. I got buggered up a few times but thought I escaped pretty good. Now I wake up on a rainy day and think, I remember this. I remember it right here.

A PARTICULAR LANGUAGE

When I tell Jerry stories about the racetrack he doesn't say much. It's hard for people who haven't been there to understand. There's a particular language you pick up on the track. I'd come home for the holidays and try to talk to my family, but nothing I said made sense to them. What? they'd say. Huh? What do you mean?

A racetracker doesn't say *We won a race*. A race-tracker says *We win*. It's not proper English. It's not *We won*. It's not *We will win*. The race is over, it's already won, but we say *We win, we win, we win*.

AFTERWORD

Kick the Latch is based on interviews recorded in person and by phone in 2018, 2020, and 2021. With Sonia's permission, I transcribed those recordings and used them to write this book, which is a work of fiction. My gratitude to Sonia—and to my mother, who introduced us—is profound.

Kathryn Scanlan

Daunt Books

Founded in 2010, Daunt Books Publishing grew out of Daunt Books, independent booksellers with shops in London and the south of England. We publish the finest writing in English and in translation, from literary fiction – novels and short stories – to narrative non-fiction, including essays and memoirs. Our modern classics list revives authors whose work has unjustly fallen out of print. In 2020 we launched Daunt Books Originals, an imprint for bold and inventive new writing.

www.dauntbookspublishing.co.uk